The exceptional Boss:

secrets to becoming a great leader

Sarah M. Remy

Table of contents

Introduction

Developing a Leadership Mindset

Effective Communication

Inspiring and Motivating Others

Building Trust and Authenticity

Emotional Intelligence

Decision-Making and Problem-Solving

Building High-Performing Teams

Leading Through Change

Coaching and Mentoring

Work-Life Balance

Effective Delegation

Conflict Resolution

Building a Positive Company Culture

Leading by Example

Performance Management

Strategic Thinking and Planning

Managing Remote Teams

Employee Recognition and Rewards

Workforce Diversity and Inclusion

Personal Growth and Self-Reflection

Conclusion

Introduction

"The Exceptional Boss: Secrets to Becoming a Great Leader," a revolutionary handbook intended to unleash your leadership potential and assist you on the road to becoming an outstanding boss.

Being a boss is not simply about carrying a title or maintaining a position of power. It is about motivating and encouraging people, fostering a pleasant work atmosphere, and producing extraordinary achievements. Whether you are a seasoned manager or want to lead a team, this book is your path to becoming an extraordinary boss—one who leads with integrity, vision, and compassion.

Within these pages, you will uncover the secrets that distinguish excellent bosses apart from others. We will dig into the crucial traits, abilities, and methods that can catapult you to new heights of leadership brilliance. From cultivating a leadership mentality to mastering effective communication, from building trust and honesty to inspiring and motivating your team, we will cover every component of great leadership. But this book is not only a theoretical investigation of leadership notions. It is a practical handbook that blends research-based ideas with tangible methods and real-world examples. Each chapter is filled with proven techniques, practical insights, and thought-provoking activities to help you implement the concepts of outstanding leadership in your unique setting.

As you begin on this adventure, be ready to question your preconceptions, widen your ideas, and embrace personal development. Leadership is a continual process, and this book will empower you with the skills and insight to constantly build your leadership qualities.

Keep in mind that excellent managers are not born; they are created. They are people that consistently seek self-improvement, invest in their teams, and inspire excellence in others. By the conclusion of this book, you will have the insights, knowledge, and inspiration to turn yourself into the extraordinary leader you wish to be.

Now, let's go on this revolutionary adventure together and uncover the keys to being a genuinely amazing boss.

Developing a Leadership Mindset

In the domain of leadership, the mind is everything. It establishes the framework for how leaders see and approach their responsibilities, their teams, and the difficulties they encounter. Developing a leadership mentality is not a one-time event but a continuous process that includes self-reflection, learning, and purposeful practice. In this chapter, we will discuss the significance of establishing a leadership mentality and present practical insights and techniques to foster this crucial attribute.

The Theory of a Leadership Mindset:

A leadership mentality is a collection of ideas, attitudes, and views that determine how leaders approach their job and interact with others. It is the prism through which they evaluate situations, make choices, and motivate their employees. A strong leadership attitude helps leaders to handle uncertainty, overcome barriers, and inspire greatness in others.

Embracing a Growth Mentality: At the basis of leadership, the mentality is a growth mindset—a conviction that talents and intellect can be developed through devotion and effort. Leaders with a growth mentality accept difficulties, persevere in the face of setbacks, and regard failures as opportunities for learning and progress. They urge their employees to adopt this approach, establishing a culture of constant development and innovation.

Self-Awareness and Reflection: Developing a leadership mentality needs self-awareness—the capacity to perceive and comprehend one's strengths, shortcomings, values, and prejudices. Self-reflection methods, such as blogging or soliciting feedback, assist leaders to acquire insights into their leadership style and identify growth opportunities. By knowing themselves better, leaders can make purposeful decisions that correspond with their beliefs and lead honestly.

Purpose and Vision: A leadership attitude is motivated by a strong sense of purpose and vision. Exceptional leaders develop a compelling vision that inspires and drives their employees. They tie their work to a bigger goal, enabling their colleagues to perceive the influence of their efforts. Leaders with a strong sense of purpose are more resilient in the face of setbacks and can mobilize their employees behind a common objective.

Continual Learning and flexibility: Leadership is a dynamic journey that involves continual learning and flexibility. Leaders with a growth mindset aggressively seek new information, skills, and views. They engage in their growth by reading, attending courses, finding mentors, and networking. By being interested and adaptive, leaders can manage change, capture opportunities, and motivate their employees to adopt a learning mentality.

Summary:

Developing a leadership mentality is a transforming process that demands attention and dedication. By adopting a growth mindset, practicing self-reflection, articulating purpose and vision, and emphasizing continuous learning, leaders may create a mentality that allows them to lead with impact and inspire their colleagues. Remember, having a leadership attitude is not a conclusion but a continuous process of growth and development. As you begin on this path, remain open-minded, accept obstacles, and lead with sincerity. By adopting a leadership attitude, you will unleash your full leadership potential and create a lasting beneficial influence on your team and business.

In a nutshell, adopting a leadership attitude is a crucial step in being an extraordinary boss. It empowers leaders to manage problems, motivate their people, and produce amazing achievements. By embracing the power of a growth mindset, practicing self-awareness, articulating purpose and vision, and emphasizing continuous learning, leaders can create a mentality that allows them to lead with authenticity and make a significant impact. Invest in building your leadership attitude, and watch as it improves not just your leadership talents but also the lives and careers of the people you lead.

Effective Communication

Effective communication sits at the core of effective leadership. It is a vital talent that helps leaders to connect, inspire, and influence people. In this chapter, we will examine the subtleties of good communication and present insights, techniques, and practical recommendations to help you become a skilled communicator.

The Theory of Effective Communication:

Building Trust and Rapport: Effective communication generates trust and rapport between leaders and their teams. When leaders communicate with clarity, sincerity, and empathy, they create an atmosphere of openness and transparency. Trust is the basis upon which good teams are founded, and effective communication plays a crucial role in creating and sustaining that trust.

Clear and Concise Statements: Leaders who communicate successfully can reduce complicated concepts into clear and concise statements. They explain their thoughts and ideas in a way that is readily understood by others, regardless of their experience or expertise. By communicating with clarity, leaders eliminate misconceptions and build alignment among their teams.

Active Listening: Effective communication entails active listening—giving full attention to others, attempting to comprehend their views, and expressing empathy. Leaders who actively listen provide a safe atmosphere for open debate, welcome varied opinions and develop a culture of cooperation and creativity.

Nonverbal Communication: Nonverbal indicators, such as body language, facial expressions, and tone of voice, play a key part in efficient communication. Leaders who pay attention to their nonverbal signals may boost their message's effectiveness and ensure that their verbal and nonverbal clues correspond. By exercising self-awareness and recognizing the importance of nonverbal communication, leaders can express authenticity and develop greater relationships with their employees.

Feedback and acknowledgment: Effective communication comprises the skill of offering feedback and acknowledgment. Leaders who understand the art of offering constructive criticism in a supportive and constructive way enable their team members to grow and develop. Additionally, acknowledging and appreciating the efforts of people and teams generates a pleasant and motivated work atmosphere.

Summary:

In a nutshell, effective communication is a vital talent for leaders wanting to inspire, influence, and create a great work environment. By creating trust and rapport, speaking with clarity and conciseness, practicing active listening, being sensitive to nonverbal clues, and offering feedback and acknowledgment, leaders may lift their communication skills to new heights.

Keep in mind that good communication is a two-way street that includes both speaking and listening abilities. It is not simply about conveying messages but also about understanding and engaging with people. As a leader, devote time and effort to improving your communication skills, seek criticism, and continually try to improve.

By mastering the art of effective communication, you will strengthen your leadership skills, develop deeper connections with your team members, and achieve more success in your professional activities. Effective communication is a strong instrument that, when used with purpose and expertise, can impact not just your leadership path but also the lives of those you guide.

Inspiring and Motivating Others

As a leader, one of your key roles is to inspire and drive your team members to attain their maximum potential. The capacity to generate passion, drive, and dedication in others is a characteristic of excellent leadership. In this chapter, we will dig into the art of inspiring and motivating others, covering tactics, techniques, and ideas that can help you become a catalyst for excellence within your team.

Understanding Motivation:

Motivation is the driving force behind people's behaviors, activities, and performance. It is a complicated interaction of innate and external elements that differ from person to person. As a leader, knowing the varied motivating drives of your team members is crucial to unleashing their potential and building a high-performance culture.

Creating a Compelling Vision: A compelling vision is a strong tool for inspiring and motivating people. By clearly defining a vision that connects with their goals, values, and sense of purpose, leaders may establish a shared sense of direction and purpose throughout the team. A well-crafted vision acts as a beacon of inspiration and generates intrinsic motivation, inspiring team members to go above and beyond to accomplish amazing achievements.

Providing Meaningful Work: People are innately motivated by the need for meaningful work that resonates with their beliefs and helps them to make a difference. Leaders who create opportunities for team members to participate in important initiatives, contribute their unique abilities and see the effect of their effort are more likely to inspire motivation and commitment. By tying individual tasks and duties to the wider mission of the team and company, leaders may generate a feeling of pride and satisfaction.

Fostering a pleasant Work atmosphere: A pleasant work atmosphere is a fertile ground for motivation and inspiration. Leaders who establish an environment of trust, respect, and psychological safety inspire open communication, cooperation, and creativity. Celebrating victories, offering support, and acknowledging the efforts and contributions of team members enhance morale and drive employees to work at their best.

Empowering and Developing Others: Empowerment and development go hand in hand with inspiration and motivation. Leaders that empower their team members by distributing authority, allowing autonomy, and fostering decision-making promote a feeling of ownership and accountability. Additionally, investing in the growth and development of people via coaching, mentoring, and learning opportunities boosts their talents and feeds their desire to achieve.

Communicating and Connecting: Effective communication is a strong tool for inspiring and motivating people. Leaders that communicate with clarity, sincerity, and empathy connect on a deeper level with their team members. By listening actively, giving assistance, and providing constructive criticism, leaders display their genuine interest in the development and success of their team members, promoting motivation and a feeling of belonging.

Summary:

In a nutshell, inspiring and motivating people is a crucial talent for leaders who aim to develop a high-performance culture and accomplish outstanding outcomes. By establishing a compelling vision, offering meaningful work, promoting a great work environment, empowering and developing people, and communicating and connecting effectively, leaders may light the fire of inspiration inside their teams.

Keep in mind that inspiring and encouraging people is not a one-time activity but a continuous commitment. It takes a deep awareness of people's motivating drives, empathy, and the capacity to change your leadership style to match their requirements. By consistently investing in your team members' development, offering support and recognition, and leading with honesty and enthusiasm, you will inspire and drive them to attain new heights of success.

As a leader, your capacity to inspire and encourage others has the potential to alter people, teams, and organizations. By honing this talent, you become a catalyst for good change and create an atmosphere where brilliance grows.

Building Trust and Authenticity

Trust and sincerity constitute the core of good leadership. When leaders emphasize creating trust and authenticity among their teams, they create an atmosphere that supports collaboration, open communication, and high performance. In this chapter, we will discuss the significance of creating trust and authenticity as a leader and present practical ideas and techniques to foster these vital attributes.

The Importance of Trust:

Trust is the cornerstone of successful relationships and efficient cooperation. When trust is there, team members feel secure to express themselves, take chances, and provide their best efforts. Trust helps people to cooperate, share ideas, and work towards a shared objective with confidence and dedication.

Leading by Example: Leaders must lead by example and exhibit trustworthiness in their actions and words. When leaders continuously behave with integrity, honesty, and openness, they create a standard that team members may mimic. By upholding agreements, acknowledging errors, and acting responsibly, leaders develop credibility and provide the framework for trust to thrive.

Active Listening and Empathy: Active listening is a valuable skill for creating trust. When leaders listen carefully and empathetically, they exhibit their genuine interest in understanding others' viewpoints and needs. By expressing empathy, leaders establish a safe atmosphere for open communication, affirm others' perspectives, and develop a feeling of belonging.

Transparency and Open Communication: Transparent and open communication is vital for creating confidence among teams. Leaders who speak honestly, provide information, and offer context behind choices foster an atmosphere of trust and eliminate ambiguity. Transparent leaders promote inquiries, solicit criticism, and provide chances for debate, establishing a culture of trust and cooperation.

Consistency and dependability: Consistency and dependability are crucial aspects of creating confidence. Leaders that regularly follow through on pledges, fulfill deadlines, and deliver on promises develop a reputation for dependability. When team members can depend on their leader's words and actions, trust grows, and the team becomes more cohesive and successful.

The Essence of Authenticity:

Authenticity is the congruence between one's words, actions, values, and beliefs. Authentic leaders create an environment of trust and inspire others via their honest and open attitudes. When leaders exemplify authenticity, they offer a safe place for team members to be their genuine selves, fostering creativity, innovation, and personal development.

Knowing Yourself: Authentic leadership starts with self-awareness. Leaders who understand their beliefs, talents, limitations, and motivations are better suited to lead with authenticity. By understanding themselves, leaders may connect their behaviors with their genuine selves and develop credibility with their team members.

Embracing weakness: Authentic leaders are not afraid to demonstrate weakness and recognize when they don't have all the answers. By recognizing their shortcomings and soliciting opinions from others, leaders create an environment of psychological safety. When team members witness their leader being honest and vulnerable, they feel comfortable doing the same, establishing stronger ties and trust.

Honoring distinctiveness: Authentic leaders embrace and celebrate the distinctiveness of their team members. They acknowledge that a variety of ideas, backgrounds, and experiences strengthens the team's collective intellect. By fostering an inclusive workplace that honors and respects all opinions, genuine leaders empower their team members to bring their complete selves to work.

Consistency and Congruence: Consistency and congruence are vital for true leadership. Leaders who constantly connect their words and actions with their values and beliefs generate a feeling of honesty and reliability. Authentic leaders are honest in their relationships and stay true to themselves even in hard conditions.

Summary:

In a nutshell, developing trust and sincerity is important to successful leadership. By leading by example, exercising active listening and empathy, supporting openness and open communication, and embodying authenticity, leaders may build an atmosphere of trust, and cooperation.

Emotional Intelligence

Emotional intelligence (EI) is a vital talent for leaders looking to negotiate the intricacies of human relationships and motivate high-performance teams. It comprises the capacity to detect, analyze, and control emotions—both one's own and those of others. In this chapter, we will discuss the role of emotional intelligence in leadership and present practical insights and ways to build and grow this vital trait.

The Theory of Emotional Intelligence:

Self-Awareness: Self-awareness is the cornerstone of emotional intelligence. Leaders with high EI have a profound grasp of their own emotions, strengths, limitations, and triggers. They are in sync with their emotions, helping them to manage their actions and react properly to diverse circumstances. Self-awareness empowers leaders to make deliberate decisions, handle stress efficiently, and develop meaningful connections with others.

Empathy and Understanding: Empathy is a basic component of emotional intelligence. Leaders that exhibit empathy may comprehend and share the sentiments of others. They can put themselves in others' shoes and appreciate the viewpoints and requirements of their team members. By displaying empathy, leaders develop trust, enhance relationships, and promote a supportive and inclusive work environment.

Relationship Management: Emotionally intelligent leaders succeed at relationship management. They negotiate disagreements, promote cooperation, and develop deep ties with their team members. Leaders with high EI communicate well, actively listen, and adjust their communication approach to various persons. They are adept at influencing and motivating people, resolving disagreements, and creating a positive team dynamic.

Resilience: Emotional intelligence gives leaders the resilience to bounce back from failures and negotiate hard circumstances. Leaders with high EI can manage their emotions, stay cool under pressure, and make informed judgments. They can deal with stress, tolerate uncertainty, and encourage their colleagues to remain focused and motivated through challenging circumstances.

Building Emotional Intelligence:

Self-Reflection and Self-Development: Self-reflection is a strong technique for building emotional intelligence. Leaders might participate in introspection, writing, or requesting feedback to obtain insights into their emotions, actions, and influence on others. By committing to personal growth and development, leaders may strengthen their emotional intelligence and become more successful in their leadership positions.

Practice Empathy: Empathy may be created through practice and intentionality. Leaders may actively attempt to comprehend others' viewpoints, listen with an open mind, and display empathy in their interactions. By exhibiting real care and regard for their team members' feelings and experiences, leaders develop a culture of empathy and create a supportive and trustworthy atmosphere.

Build Self-Regulation: Self-regulation is the capacity to regulate and control one's emotions. Leaders may build self-regulation by exercising strategies such as deep breathing, mindfulness, and emotional awareness. By stopping before responding, analyzing the repercussions of their actions, and selecting answers that correspond with their beliefs and aims, leaders may develop their self-regulation abilities.

Continuous Learning: Emotional intelligence is a lifetime process of learning and development. Leaders may participate in continual learning through reading books, taking seminars, finding mentors, and practicing self-reflection. By keeping interested and open-minded, leaders may improve their emotional intelligence and adjust their leadership techniques to diverse circumstances and personalities.

Summary:

In a nutshell, emotional intelligence is a vital talent for leaders who aspire to develop good connections, motivate their employees, and handle problems efficiently. By gaining self-awareness, exercising empathy, mastering relationship management, and fostering resilience, leaders may strengthen their emotional intelligence and have a major influence on their teams and companies.

Keep in mind that emotional intelligence is not a permanent attribute but a talent that can be cultivated and perfected through time. As a leader, engage in your emotional intelligence by participating in self-reflection, exercising empathy, and creating self-regulation.

Decision-Making and Problem-Solving

Effective decision-making and problem-solving are key abilities for leaders in today's complicated and fast-changing corporate scene. Leaders that exhibit the capacity to make informed judgments and solve issues effectively may traverse hurdles, grasp opportunities, and drive organizational success. In this chapter, we will discuss the role of decision-making and problem-solving in leadership and present practical insights and techniques to strengthen these vital qualities.

The Significance of Decision-Making:

Strategic Alignment: Decision-making plays a critical role in aligning activities with the organization's strategic objectives. Leaders who make well-informed judgments based on a clear grasp of the organization's vision and goals may lead their teams on the correct path. Strategic decision-making helps leaders to deploy resources efficiently, prioritize activities, and develop a unified and focused staff.

Risk Management: Decision-making requires analyzing risks and making decisions that limit possible negative effects. Effective leaders examine risks, obtain pertinent information, and consider choices before making educated decisions. By analyzing possible risks and benefits, leaders may negotiate uncertainty and make choices that optimize results while reducing potential problems.

Innovation and development: Leaders that adopt a proactive decision-making approach generate a culture of innovation and development. They urge their staff to think critically, question the existing quo, and explore new ideas. By allowing people to make choices and take measured risks, leaders create an atmosphere that supports innovation, learning, and continual progress.

The Technique of Problem-Solving:

Define the Problem: Effective problem-solving starts with clearly describing the issue or task at hand. Leaders that take the time to understand the core reasons, obtain relevant data, and ask probing questions may uncarth insights and propose viable solutions. By clearly describing the issue, leaders may concentrate their efforts on developing acceptable and lasting solutions.

Analyze possibilities: Leaders engage in critical thinking and analysis to examine numerous possibilities and possible solutions. They analyze many views, balance the benefits and drawbacks, and assess the feasibility, effect, and risks connected with each alternative. By obtaining feedback from team members, subject matter experts, and stakeholders, leaders may make better-informed choices and determine the best feasible solution.

collective Approach: Problem-solving is generally a collective activity. Leaders include their team members in the process, promoting varied opinions and developing a feeling of ownership and responsibility. By supporting a collaborative approach, leaders tap into the combined wisdom and creativity of the team, resulting in more robust ideas and higher commitment to execution.

Decision Implementation: Effective problem-solving doesn't stop with decision-making; it entails translating choices into action. Leaders construct implementation strategies, allocate roles, and set clear timetables and objectives. They communicate choices effectively, ensuring that team members understand their roles and responsibilities. Through successful implementation, leaders ensure that choices are put into practice, monitored, and altered as appropriate.

Enhancing Decision-Making and Problem-Solving Skills:

Data-Driven Decision-Making: Leaders may increase their decision-making abilities by adopting a data-driven strategy. They acquire and evaluate relevant data, harness technology and analytics, and seek evidence-based insights. Data-driven decision-making empowers leaders to make more objective and informed decisions, decreasing biases and boosting the chance of successful results.

Continual Learning: Decision-making and problem-solving are abilities that may be developed via continual learning and practice. Leaders should explore chances to enhance their expertise, remain current on industry trends, and learn from their experiences. By reflecting on prior mistakes, accepting criticism, and seeking to mentor, leaders may strengthen their decision-making and problem-solving aptitude.

Risk-Taking and Learning from Failure: Leaders must be ready to take measured chances and learn from failure. They foster an atmosphere where errors are recognized as learning opportunities and where experimentation and creativity are appreciated. By having a development mentality, leaders establish a culture.

Building High-Performing Teams

Building a high-performing team is a vital job of a leader. High-performing teams are defined by cooperation, trust, shared objectives, and a strong sense of responsibility. As a leader, your ability to create an atmosphere that supports high performance and allows employees to attain their full potential is vital. In this chapter, we will discuss the relevance of developing high-performing teams and present practical insights and ways to create and maintain such teams.

The Importance of High-Performing Teams:

Enhanced Productivity: High-performing teams continuously offer great outcomes. When people join together with a common objective, defined responsibilities, and successful teamwork, their combined effort enhances their output. High-performing teams harness the capabilities of each team member, capitalize on varied viewpoints, and work synergistically toward attaining corporate goals.

Innovation and Creativity: Teams that function at a high-performance level establish an atmosphere that supports innovation and creativity. When team members feel psychologically comfortable and empowered to voice their views, they are more likely to provide unique insights and viewpoints. A culture of innovation among high-performing teams promotes continual learning, flexibility, and the production of novel solutions.

Employee Engagement and Contentment: High-performing teams encourage employee engagement and contentment. When employees feel respected, challenged, and supported within their team, they are more likely to be motivated and devoted to their tasks. High-performing teams create opportunities for development, recognition, and significant contributions, building a good work environment that attracts and keeps top people.

The main factors in Building High-Performing Teams:

Clear Vision and Objectives: Leaders must present a clear vision and develop objectives that motivate and lead the team. By defining a compelling direction, leaders generate a feeling of purpose and concentration that aligns individual efforts toward a common objective. Clear objectives give clarity and direction, helping team members to understand their duties and prioritize their work successfully.

Trust and Psychological Safety: Trust is the basis of high-performing teams. Leaders must establish a culture of trust by supporting open communication, openness, and sincerity. When team members trust one another and feel psychologically comfortable, they are more inclined to take chances, share ideas, and offer constructive criticism. Trust enables healthy dispute resolution, cooperation, and creativity within the team.

Effective Communication: Effective communication is crucial for developing high-performing teams. Leaders should build channels for open and transparent communication, ensuring that information flows easily inside the team. Unambiguous communication helps align expectations, manage problems, and keep team members informed. Leaders should encourage active listening, seek varied ideas, and foster healthy discourse.

Role Clarity and Alignment: High-performing teams demand clarity in roles and responsibilities. Leaders should ensure that team members understand their specific duties and how they contribute to the team's broader goals. By connecting individual qualities and abilities with particular tasks, leaders optimize each team member's potential and generate a feeling of ownership and responsibility.

Collaboration and Teamwork: Collaboration is the basis of high-performing teams. Leaders should establish a collaborative atmosphere where team members work together towards common objectives. Encouraging cross-functional cooperation, boosting information sharing, and supporting teamwork activities fosters relationships among team members and increases overall performance.

Sustaining High-Performing Teams:

Continued growth: Leaders must invest in the continual growth of their team members. By offering chances for learning, training, and skill development, leaders enable team members to increase their talents and attain their full potential. Continuous development ensures that high-performing teams adapt to changing demands and stay competitive.

Recognition and Rewards: Acknowledging and appreciating the successes and efforts of team members is vital for keeping a high-performing team. Leaders should offer frequent feedback, acknowledge victories, and reward highly.

Leading Through Change

Transition is a constant in today's dynamic corporate world, and good leadership through times of transition is vital for organizational success. Leaders who can negotiate change with clarity, empathy, and resilience encourage their people to adapt, innovate, and prosper. In this chapter, we will discuss the relevance of leading during change and present practical insights and ways to lead successfully through moments of transition and uncertainty.

The Importance of Leading Through Change:

Managing Resistance: Change typically inspires resistance and anxiety among employees within an organization. Leaders who can successfully lead through change can lessen opposition and allow a smoother transition. By providing clear information, resolving concerns, and integrating team members in the change process, leaders develop trust and lessen resistance, allowing the business to accept change more quickly.

developing flexibility: Leading through change entails developing flexibility within the company. Leaders that cultivate a growth attitude, promote learning and development and enable people to accept change as an opportunity establish a culture of adaptation. By promoting adaptation, leaders help their employees to overcome uncertainty, embrace new ways of working, and remain ahead in a continuously dynamic business world.

Inspiring Resilience: Change may be tough and demanding, leading to stress and uncertainty. Leaders that lead through change build resilience in their employees. By displaying their resilience, giving support and resources, and encouraging self-care and well-being, leaders help people to bounce back from setbacks and sustain high levels of performance and motivation throughout times of transition.

Key Principles for Leading Through Change:

Communicate with Clarity: Clear and consistent communication is crucial during times of transition. Leaders must convey the reasons for change, the intended objectives, and the effect on people and the company. By delivering clear and timely information, leaders remove uncertainty, resolve issues, and keep the team informed throughout the transition process.

Lead with Empathy: Leading with empathy is vital during times of transition. Leaders must understand and respect the feelings and concerns of their team members. By actively listening, displaying empathy, and giving assistance, leaders create a safe and supportive atmosphere that promotes trust and helps people negotiate the emotional hurdles involved with change.

Involve and Empower: Involving and empowering team members in the transformation process encourages ownership and commitment. Leaders should request opinions, engage staff in decision-making, and assign duties to enable people to participate in the change process. By incorporating team members, leaders tap into their collective wisdom, boost engagement, and create a feeling of shared responsibility for the results.

offer Support and Resources: During change, leaders must offer the necessary support and resources to allow their teams to succeed. This involves training, mentoring, and coaching to help people gain the skills and competencies necessary for the transition. By providing the necessary support and resources, leaders help their teams to handle the obstacles of change successfully and boost their chances of success.

Lead by Example: Leaders must lead by example and embody the required behaviors and attitudes throughout the transformation. By displaying adaptation, resilience, and a positive attitude, leaders motivate their staff to follow suit. Leading by example reinforces the words expressed and indicates the leaders' commitment to the change, encouraging trust and confidence in the team.

Leading Through Complex Change:

Anticipate and strategy: Complex change generally demands a complete strategy. Leaders should foresee possible problems, risks, and opportunities related to the transition and establish a well-thought-out strategy that tackles these elements. By designing a plan, leaders give clarity, direction, and structure throughout a complicated transition, enabling their employees to navigate through complexity.

Foster Collaboration and Alignment: Complex transformation generally includes several stakeholders and interconnected processes. Leaders must create cooperation and alignment across multiple teams and departments. By developing platforms for cooperation, facilitating cross-functional communication, and promoting shared understanding and goals, leaders guarantee that all stakeholders are working together towards the common objectives of the change endeavor. Collaboration and alignment promote coordination, decrease disagreements, and optimize the success of the change implementation.

Monitor Progress and Adapt: Leading through complicated change needs leaders to regularly monitor progress and make appropriate modifications along the way. Leaders should set key performance indicators (KPIs) and milestones to measure the success of the transformation endeavor. Regularly monitoring the metrics, soliciting input, and being open to making modifications depending on the developing requirements and circumstances guarantee that the change project continues on track and achieves the anticipated goals.

establish Change competence: To handle difficult change effectively, leaders must establish change competence inside the company. This requires empowering people with the essential skills, information, and resources to embrace and drive change. Leaders should invest in change management training, give tools and frameworks for managing change, and promote a culture that supports continuous learning and progress. Building change capacity guarantees that the company can successfully adjust to future changes and maintain high-performance levels.

Summary:

Leading through change is a vital ability for executives in today's quickly developing corporate scene. By implementing effective techniques such as clear communication, empathy, engagement, support, and leading by example, leaders can manage change effectively and encourage their teams to adapt, innovate, and prosper. Whether the change is simple or complicated, the capacity to lead through change with resilience, empathy, and a focus on cooperation and alignment is crucial for achieving organizational success in a dynamic and ever-changing environment.

Coaching and Mentoring

Coaching and mentoring are effective leadership practices that assist the growth, development, and success of people within an organization. As a leader, your ability to teach and mentor people may have a tremendous influence on their performance, engagement, and career growth. In this chapter, we will discuss the role of coaching and mentoring in leadership and present practical insights and ways to successfully coach and mentor people to attain their full potential.

The Significance of Coaching and Mentoring:

Individual Growth and Development: Coaching and mentoring offer opportunity for people to increase their skills, knowledge, and capacities. By giving direction, feedback, and support, leaders allow employees to overcome problems, acquire new abilities, and broaden their professional horizons. Coaching and mentoring build a culture of continual learning, personal growth, and professional development inside the business.

Talent Development and Retention: Coaching and mentoring assist in the development and retention of elite talent. When leaders devote time and effort to coaching and mentoring their team members, they show a commitment to their development and success. This generates loyalty, motivation, and a feeling of belonging, lowering turnover and recruiting high-potential workers to the business.

Leadership Pipeline: Coaching and mentoring play a critical role in producing future leaders. By coaching and mentoring people, leaders recognize and foster emerging potential, preparing them for leadership responsibilities. Coaching and mentoring programs provide a healthy leadership pipeline, guaranteeing a seamless transfer of leadership and continuity in the organization's performance.

Key Principles for Effective Coaching and Mentoring:

Establish Trust and Rapport: Coaching and mentoring relationships thrive on trust and rapport. Leaders must establish a secure and supportive atmosphere where people feel comfortable discussing their aims, concerns, and ambitions. By creating trust, actively listening, and displaying empathy, leaders provide a basis for successful coaching and mentoring.

Set Clear Goals and Expectations: Clear goals and expectations give a framework for teaching and mentoring. Leaders should engage cooperatively with employees to develop relevant and realistic goals that match their ambitions and the organization's objectives. Clear expectations help people remain focused, motivated, and responsible for their growth.

Active Listening and Feedback: Active listening is a vital ability for successful coaching and mentoring. Leaders should listen intently, ask probing questions, and endeavor to understand the viewpoints and needs of the persons they are coaching or mentoring. Providing constructive and timely feedback helps people acquire self-awareness, discover areas for improvement, and take measures toward progress.

Tailor Coaching and Mentoring Approaches:
Every person is unique, and coaching and mentoring practices should be adapted to their particular requirements and preferences. Leaders should consider people's learning styles, strengths, and growth areas while establishing coaching and mentoring tactics. By tailoring techniques, leaders ensure that coaching and mentoring interactions are engaging, relevant, and effective.

stimulate Self-Reflection and Learning: Coaching and mentoring should stimulate self-reflection and create a development mentality. Leaders should encourage people to reflect on their experiences, learn from achievements and disappointments, and explore chances for self-improvement. By building a culture of continual learning and self-development, leaders encourage people to take control of their paths.

Provide Support and Resources: Effective coaching and mentoring include giving the essential support and resources for people's growth. Leaders should give direction, share relevant information and resources, and link people with learning opportunities and networks. By offering assistance, leaders demonstrate their commitment to the people's achievement and empower them with the skills they need to succeed.

Mentoring in contrast to Coaching:

It's vital to differentiate between coaching and mentoring. While coaching focuses on particular objectives, performance improvement, and skill development, mentoring is more focused on general career counseling, long-term growth, and exchanging experiences.

Both coaching and mentoring techniques have their role in leadership development and supporting people's progress.

Coaching: Coaching is often short-term and goal-oriented. It focuses on particular abilities, habits, or performance areas that people need to acquire or improve. The coach works as a facilitator, helping clients increase self-awareness, explore other views, and establish action plans to attain their objectives. Coaching sessions are frequently planned, with specified goals and timetables.

Coaching is especially beneficial when people seek assistance in areas such as skill growth, problem-solving, decision-making, or conquering specific problems. It offers focused coaching, feedback, and accountability to help people achieve progress toward their objectives.

Mentoring: Mentoring, on the other hand, is a long-term connection centered on overall professional development and personal improvement. Mentors, who are generally more experienced professionals, give guidance, advice, and support based on their own experiences and expertise.

Mentoring relationships may persist over a longer time, providing strong bonds and continuing support.

Mentoring is beneficial when people want wider counsel, career assistance, and exposure to diverse ideas and experiences. Mentors give insights about negotiating organizational dynamics, creating networks, and making smart career choices. They give a secure area for mentees to explore their objectives, seek direction, and receive insight from their mentor's experience.

Summary:

Coaching and mentoring are effective leadership practices that contribute to individual growth, talent development, and organizational success. Effective coaching and mentoring entail developing trust, having clear objectives, active listening, offering feedback, and personalizing techniques to fit people's distinct needs.
By coaching and mentoring people, leaders build a culture of continuous learning, enable individuals to attain their greatest potential and establish a strong leadership pipeline. Both coaching and mentoring techniques have their place in leadership development, complementing one another to

create a complete and powerful support structure for people's growth and achievement.

Work-Life Balance

Work-life balance is a vital feature of contemporary living, especially in today's fast-paced and stressful work situations. Achieving a good work-life balance is vital for people to preserve their general well-being, boost productivity, and develop meaningful connections. In this chapter, we will discuss the relevance of work-life balance and present practical ideas and solutions to help people integrate their personal and professional lives efficiently.

The Importance of Work-Life Balance:

Well-being and Health: Work-life balance is crucial for preserving physical, mental, and emotional well-being. When people have time for rest, relaxation, and self-care, they enjoy reduced stress levels, enhanced mental health, and higher general contentment with life. Striking a balance between work and personal life helps people to recharge, participate in activities they like, and take care of their physical and emotional needs.

Enhanced Productivity and Performance: A good work-life balance significantly influences productivity and performance. When people have time to participate in things outside of work, such as hobbies, exercise, and spending quality time with loved ones, they sense higher contentment and motivation. This, in turn, translates into enhanced attention, inventiveness, and efficiency when people are involved in their tasks. Achieving work-life balance helps people to contribute their best selves to both their personal and professional endeavors.

Relationships and Social ties: Work-life balance is vital for cultivating meaningful relationships and building social ties. Spending quality time with family, friends, and loved ones is vital for creating strong ties and maintaining a support system. When people emphasize their connections, they enjoy a better sense of belonging and satisfaction in their life, which favorably influences their overall well-being and happiness.

Methods for Achieving Work-Life Balance:

Set Priorities: Start by identifying your priorities in both your personal and professional life. Identify what is important to you and what provides you pleasure and contentment. By matching your behaviors with your priorities, you may make conscious decisions that encourage work-life balance.

Establish Boundaries: Create clear boundaries between work and personal life. Set specified hours for work, and when those hours are finished, intentionally unplug from job-related activities. Avoid bringing work into your time and vice versa. Establishing boundaries helps establish a feeling of separation and enables you to fully participate in both aspects of your life.

Practice Time Management: Effectively manage your time by prioritizing work, establishing realistic deadlines, and delegating when required. Learn to say no to non-essential engagements that may damage your work-life balance. By planning your time wisely, you may assign distinct intervals for business and leisure interests, ensuring you have adequate time for both.

Foster Flexibility: Explore chances for flexibility in your work arrangements. Speak with your company or supervisor about possibilities such as flexible working hours, remote work, or shortened work weeks. Flexibility helps you to better combine professional and personal duties, resulting in enhanced work-life balance.

Take Care of Yourself: Self-care is vital for preserving work-life balance. Prioritize activities that enhance physical and mental well-being, such as exercise, a good diet, relaxation methods, and sufficient sleep. When you prioritize self-care, you have more energy and attention to dedicate to both work and personal life.

Delegate and Seek Support: Recognize that you don't have to accomplish everything on your own. Delegate duties, both at work and in your personal life, to spread the burden and free up time for other priorities. Seek help from coworkers, family members, or friends when required. Asking for assistance is not a sign of weakness but a wise technique for keeping balance and preventing burnout.

Unplug and disengage: Take frequent breaks from technology and disengage from work-related gadgets. Designate distinct hours throughout your day or week when you purposefully unplug emails, alerts, and work-related tasks. Use this time to indulge in activities that help you relax, refuel, and concentrate on your personal life.

convey and Negotiate: Openly convey your work-life balance demands with your employer, coworkers, and loved ones. Discuss your limits, availability, and expectations to ensure that everyone is aware of your priorities. Negotiate mutually advantageous agreements that promote your work-life balance, such as flexible scheduling or alternate work arrangements.

Practice Mindfulness: Incorporate mindfulness techniques into your routine. Mindfulness helps you remain present, manage stress, and find a balance between the pressures of work and personal life. Set aside time for meditation, deep breathing exercises, or just being present in the moment.

Regularly Evaluate and Adjust: Work-life balance is not a one-time success but a continuous journey. Regularly examine your work-life balance and make modifications as required. Assess if your priorities and limits are still aligned with your present circumstances and make necessary adjustments to guarantee continuous balance.

Summary:

Achieving work-life balance is a constant process that demands intentional effort and frequent review. By prioritizing your well-being, establishing boundaries, managing your time wisely, and seeking help, you can combine your personal and professional life in a manner that fosters satisfaction, productivity, and overall pleasure. Remember, work-life balance looks different for everyone, so it's crucial to define what it means to you and build a balance that corresponds with your beliefs and objectives. By emphasizing work-life balance, you may lead to a more peaceful, joyful, and successful existence.

Effective Delegation

Delegation is a vital ability for effective leaders. It entails allocating duties and responsibilities to others, allowing people to take ownership and contribute to the fulfillment of company objectives. Effective delegation not only helps leaders manage their workload but also encourages the growth of team members, boosts productivity, and builds a culture of trust and cooperation. In this chapter, we will discuss the relevance of successful delegation and present practical insights and ways to develop this key leadership ability.

The Importance of Effective Delegation:

Workload Management: Delegation helps leaders to spread tasks and responsibilities across team members, helping manage their workload efficiently. By sharing duties, leaders may concentrate on high-priority and strategic activities that need their skills, while simultaneously ensuring that regular and operational chores are handled effectively. Effective delegation ensures that work is handled fairly and avoids leaders from being overwhelmed or burned out.

Skill Development: Delegation allows team members to grow their skills, knowledge, and capacities. When leaders assign duties to team members, they offer them an opportunity to acquire new skills, take on more demanding responsibilities, and widen their experience. This encourages continual learning, professional progress, and career advancement within the team.

Empowerment and Engagement: Delegation empowers team members by entrusting them with important duties. When people are given autonomy and responsibility over their job, they feel respected, trusted, and inspired to perform at their best. Effective delegation generates a feeling of ownership, responsibility, and engagement among team members, leading to enhanced work satisfaction and commitment.

Team Collaboration and Efficiency: Delegation facilitates collaboration and teamwork inside the company. By including team members in decision-making and task execution, leaders foster a culture of communal effort and shared accountability. Effective delegation promotes communication, collaboration, and efficiency among team members, as they work together towards shared objectives.

Techniques for Effective Delegation:

Assign responsibilities Appropriately: Understand the talents, skills, and capacities of your team members before allocating responsibilities. Match tasks to personnel who have the required abilities and expertise to handle them efficiently. Consider their interests, growth objectives, and ability to take on extra duties. Assigning duties correctly puts team members up for success and optimizes their potential.

Clearly Define Expectations: When distributing work, be upfront and detailed about the anticipated deliverables, quality standards, and timeframes. Clearly express your expectations, ensuring that team members understand what needs to be completed and the degree of performance required. This clarity helps minimize misunderstandings and ensures that work is performed to the appropriate quality.

Provide Adequate Resources and Support: Ensure that team members have access to the resources, tools, and information they need to accomplish allocated responsibilities effectively. Provide appropriate training, advice, and support to assist them overcome any issues or barriers they may experience.

Be accessible for inquiries, give comments, and provide support as required during the delegation process.

Foster Two-Way Communication: Establish open and transparent communication channels when distributing duties. Encourage team members to raise questions, seek explanations, and offer updates on their progress. Be attentive to their opinions, thoughts, and recommendations, building a collaborative atmosphere where everyone feels comfortable offering their insights and views.

Trust and Empower: Trust your team members to achieve outcomes and empower them to make choices within their given roles. Avoid micromanaging or taking back responsibilities after they have been outsourced. Trusting your team members' talents improves their confidence, enhances their feeling of ownership, and helps them to develop and flourish in their jobs.

Provide Recognition and Feedback: Recognize and acknowledge the efforts and successes of team members who have successfully fulfilled allocated duties. Offer constructive criticism to help them improve their performance and develop professionally. Celebrate their triumphs and give continuing support and direction to guarantee their sustained growth and drive.

Monitor status and offer help: Stay updated about the status of allocated tasks and offer appropriate help along the way. Regularly check in with team members to evaluate their progress, discuss any problems they may be encountering, and give support if required. By monitoring progress, you can verify that activities are on schedule and give timely advice or revisions as necessary.

Learn from Delegation Experiences: Reflect on your delegation experiences to constantly improve your approach. Assess the results, identify what worked well, and highlight opportunities for improvement. Learn from both successful and poor delegation instances to enhance your delegation abilities and adjust your approach to diverse team members and scenarios.

Summary:

Effective delegation is a vital skill for leaders to learn. By distributing duties and responsibilities, leaders not only manage their workload but also empower and grow their team members. Through successful delegation, leaders create cooperation, engagement, and productivity among their teams, while also offering chances for individual development and progress. By allocating tasks correctly, outlining expectations clearly, providing resources and support, promoting two-way communication, trusting and empowering team members, and delivering appreciation and feedback, leaders may assure the effectiveness of their delegation initiatives. Embracing good delegation methods helps to create a healthy work atmosphere, promotes team performance, and ultimately drives corporate success.

Conflict Resolution

Conflict is an unavoidable component of human contact, especially inside the workplace. As a leader, the ability to successfully settle disagreements is vital for maintaining a pleasant work environment, creating good connections, and assuring the productivity and well-being of your team members. In this chapter, we will discuss the significance of conflict resolution and present practical tactics and ways to confront and resolve problems constructively and collaboratively.

The Importance of Conflict Resolution:

Improved Relationships: Conflict resolution plays a significant part in developing relationships among team members. By handling disputes swiftly and effectively, leaders may avoid differences from growing into long-standing grudges or poisonous dynamics. Resolving disagreements helps create trust, respect, and understanding among team members, providing a healthy and cohesive work environment.

Enhanced Collaboration and Productivity: Conflict typically limits effective collaboration and decreases productivity. By handling disagreements in a timely way, leaders may foster open communication, cooperation, and idea-sharing among their teams. Resolving disagreements helps team members to concentrate on their jobs and objectives, resulting in higher productivity and the successful completion of projects.

Personal and Professional Development: Conflict resolution gives chances for personal and professional development. When disagreements are handled successfully, team members learn to voice their perspectives assertively, actively listen to others, and identify common ground for settlement. Engaging in the resolution process helps people to strengthen their communication, negotiating, and problem-solving abilities, boosting their overall effectiveness as professionals.

Retention and Employee Satisfaction: Conflict left unresolved may lead to unhappiness, tension, and disengagement among team members. Conversely, when disagreements are handled and resolved, workers feel valued and supported, leading to improved job satisfaction and increased retention rates. Effective dispute resolution helps to a strong work culture where workers feel heard, appreciated, and driven to do their best.

Techniques for Conflict Resolution:

Address disagreements Early: Address disagreements as soon as they emerge to avoid them from growing and inflicting greater harm. Encourage open communication and establish a safe environment for team members to voice their issues and perspectives. Early action provides for a fast resolution and reduces the negative influence on individuals and the team as a whole.

Foster Active Listening: Promote active listening during dispute resolution. Encourage team members to listen intently to each other without interruption, striving to grasp the underlying problems and emotions involved. Active listening helps generate empathy, decreases misconceptions, and sets the framework for good communication and resolution.

Seek similar Ground: Identify similar aims or interests that might serve as a foundation for settling. Encourage team members to look past their differences and concentrate on common goals. By identifying common ground, you may move the emphasis from individual perspectives to collaborative problem-solving, improving the resolution process.

urge cooperation: Emphasize cooperation and urge team members to work together to discover mutually acceptable solutions. Create a collaborative atmosphere where people may share ideas, explore alternative viewpoints, and participate in the resolution process. Collaborative problem-solving increases buy-in and ownership of the solutions, leading to more lasting results.

Use Effective Communication: Promote clear and constructive communication during dispute resolution. Encourage people to communicate their opinions and emotions assertively while preserving respect for others. Discourage blame or personal attacks and instead concentrate on solving the problems at hand. Effective communication ensures that issues are handled directly, with a focus on finding solutions.

Utilize Mediation and Facilitation strategies: In complicated or escalating confrontations, try applying mediation or facilitation strategies. A neutral third party may assist steer the settlement process, assuring impartiality, objectivity, and a balanced exchange of views. Mediators or facilitators may assist control emotions, foster good dialogue, and lead the parties towards a mutually satisfying outcome.

Explore Win-Win Solutions: Encourage the investigation of win-win solutions that meet the interests of all parties concerned. Instead of concentrating on a win-lose attitude, seek remedies that fulfill the interests and requirements of all persons. This collaborative approach generates a feeling of justice, encourages collaboration, and improves connections among team members.

Practice Emotional Intelligence: Emotional intelligence plays a significant part in conflict resolution. Leaders should be conscious of their own emotions and control them well throughout the resolution process. Additionally, they should be sensitive to the feelings of others, displaying empathy and understanding. By exhibiting emotional intelligence, leaders may create a supportive climate that facilitates open communication and productive problem-solving.

Encourage Continuous input: After disagreements are addressed, encourage team members to offer input on the resolution process and results. This input enables ongoing growth and learning. By knowing the opinions and experiences of team members, leaders may modify their conflict resolution tactics and create a more effective and inclusive work environment.

Follow-Up and assistance: Once a problem is settled, it is crucial to give continued assistance and follow-up. Check-in with team members to confirm that the resolution is being implemented properly and that any remaining problems or concerns are resolved. Offering assistance and monitoring progress helps sustain the good results of conflict resolution and prevents additional disputes from occurring.

Summary:

Conflict resolution is a vital talent for leaders to develop. By handling disagreements in a timely and constructive way, leaders may develop good connections, boost cooperation and productivity, and create a supportive work environment. Through tactics like addressing issues early, cultivating active listening, establishing common ground, encouraging cooperation, leveraging effective communication, and exploring win-win solutions, leaders may successfully settle conflicts and maintain a harmonic and productive team dynamic. By emphasizing conflict resolution, leaders contribute to the overall performance and well-being of their team and company.

Building a Positive Company Culture

A healthy business culture is vital for the success and well-being of a corporation. It covers the shared values, beliefs, attitudes, and behaviors that define the work environment and impact the relationships among workers. A strong and pleasant business culture encourages employee engagement, contentment, and productivity, and ultimately leads to the attainment of organizational objectives. In this chapter, we will dig into the significance of developing a healthy business culture and examine practical techniques to create and nurture it inside your firm.

The Importance of Building a Positive Company Culture:

Employee Engagement and Retention: A healthy corporate culture increases employee engagement and commitment. When workers experience a feeling of belonging, connection, and purpose inside the firm, they are more likely to be inspired, devoted, and loyal. A healthy culture helps recruit and retain top personnel, minimizing turnover rates and guaranteeing a steady staff.

Increased Productivity and Performance: A strong corporate culture has a direct influence on staff productivity and performance. When workers are happy, fulfilled, and connected with the organization's values and objectives, they are more inclined to go above and beyond in their job. They feel a feeling of ownership and take pleasure in their efforts, resulting in greater productivity, creativity, and overall success.

cooperation & Teamwork: Building a healthy corporate culture fosters cooperation, teamwork, and open communication among workers. When people feel appreciated and respected, they are more ready to share their ideas, work with others, and contribute to team success. A positive culture provides a friendly and inclusive workplace where varied viewpoints are encouraged and collaboration flourishes.

Employee Well-being and Contentment: A good corporate culture promotes employee well-being and contentment. It stresses work-life balance, fosters a healthy and supportive work environment, and gives opportunities for growth, development, and recognition. When workers feel cared for and supported, their overall contentment and well-being increase, resulting in better levels of engagement and performance.

Organizational Reputation: A great business culture leads to a solid organizational reputation. A workplace recognized for its good culture attracts top talent, promotes consumer trust and loyalty, and boosts its brand image. A good reputation may separate a business from its rivals and establish a favorable impression in the marketplace.

Approaches for Building a Positive Company Culture:

outline and Communicate essential Values: Clearly outline the essential values that will shape your organization's culture. Communicate these principles to all staff and ensure they are regularly reinforced in everyday operations. When workers understand and accept the fundamental values, they can align their actions and choices with them, promoting a healthy culture.

Lead by Example: Leaders play a significant role in building organizational culture. They should exemplify the appropriate attitudes and behaviors, functioning as role models for their teams. Consistently display honesty, respect, transparency, and empathy in your interactions and choices. Your actions will set the tone for the business and affect how workers view and embrace the culture.

Foster Communication and Collaboration: Create routes and platforms for open and transparent communication inside the company. Encourage workers to communicate their ideas, concerns, and criticism. Facilitate possibilities for cross-functional communication and teamwork. Effective communication and teamwork develop a feeling of belonging, deepen connections, and promote a healthy culture.

Empower and Recognize Workers: Empower workers by distributing responsibility, providing them liberty, and believing in their talents. Provide possibilities for professional growth, skill development, and progress. Recognize and recognize workers' efforts and accomplishments, commemorating victories and milestones. Empowered and valued workers are more likely to be engaged and dedicated to the business.

Promote Work-Life Balance: Value and emphasize work-life balance within the business. Encourage employees to maintain a healthy balance between their personal and professional lives. Provide flexibility in work schedules, offer wellness programs or initiatives, and support employees in managing their well-being. By promoting work-life balance, you create an environment where employees feel supported, respected, and able to bring their best selves to work.

Foster Inclusivity and Diversity: Create an inclusive and varied work atmosphere where people from various backgrounds, viewpoints, and experiences feel appreciated and respected. Embrace diversity in hiring practices and promote a culture that celebrates and harnesses the power of different voices and ideas. A varied and inclusive culture encourages innovation, creativity, and cooperation.

Encourage Continuous Learning and growth: Promote a culture of continuous learning and growth inside the company. Offer chances for workers to increase their skills, knowledge, and expertise. Support and invest in employee growth via training programs, seminars, mentoring, and coaching. Continuous learning encourages human development, engagement, and adaptation in a continuously changing work world.

Foster a Sense of Purpose: Help workers connect with the purpose and mission of the business. Communicate the significance and importance of their job in contributing to the wider objectives and vision. When workers understand the reason behind their duties, they experience a sense of meaning and satisfaction, driving their dedication and engagement.

Establish Clear Expectations and Feedback Mechanisms:
Set clear expectations for performance and conduct inside the company. Ensure that staff understand what is expected of them and offer frequent feedback to help them develop and improve. Constructive criticism and performance reviews encourage openness, responsibility, and continued progress.

Celebrate and Appreciate Success: Create a culture of celebration and gratitude. Recognize and thank workers for their successes, milestones, and contributions. Celebrate team victories and individual accomplishments to build a happy and supportive work environment. Genuine praise and celebration increase staff morale, motivation, and loyalty.

Summary:

Building a healthy business culture is a constant process that involves dedication and purposeful acts from executives and workers alike. By defining and communicating core values, leading by example, fostering communication and collaboration, empowering and recognizing employees, promoting work-life balance, embracing inclusivity and diversity, encouraging continuous learning, fostering a sense of purpose, establishing clear expectations and feedback mechanisms, and celebrating success, leaders can cultivate a positive culture that enhances employee engagement, productivity, and satisfaction. A healthy business culture not only helps individual workers but also adds to the overall performance and longevity of the corporation.

Leading by Example

Leading by example is a vital part of good leadership. It entails showing attitudes, beliefs, and deeds that inspire and drive others to follow suit. By setting a good example, leaders develop credibility, build trust, and promote a culture of excellence inside their teams and organizations. In this chapter, we will discuss the relevance of leading by example and look into practical techniques for leaders to exemplify this leadership strategy.

The Importance of Leading by Example:

Establishing Credibility: Leading by example develops credibility and authenticity as a leader. When leaders continually display the behaviors they demand from their team members, they win the respect and trust of those they lead. Credibility is vital for successful leadership since it helps leaders to influence and inspire people to accomplish shared objectives.

Inspiring and Motivating Others: Leaders that lead by example inspire and encourage their team members to achieve their best. When people watch their leader's passion, work ethic, and commitment, they are more likely to feel inspired and encouraged to mimic similar traits in their job. By embodying excellence, leaders build a healthy and high-performing work culture.

Shaping corporate Culture: Leaders have a huge effect on the corporate culture. By leading by example, they set the tone and create the values, attitudes, and behaviors that are promoted throughout the company. When leaders continually display good and ethical behaviors, they foster a culture of integrity, teamwork, and responsibility.

Building Trust and connections: Leading by example helps establish trust and good connections with team members. When leaders continuously display honesty, openness, and justice, they create an atmosphere where trust may grow. Trust is the cornerstone of good cooperation, open communication, and collaboration.

Developing Future Leaders: Leaders who lead by example inspire and nurture future leaders within their businesses. When team members experience their leader's dedication to personal growth, constant learning, and development, they are more inclined to follow suit. Leaders that model the necessary behaviors and engage in the development of their team members build a pipeline of competent and successful leaders.

Tactics for Leading by Example:

Clarify and Embody key principles: Identify the key principles that are vital to your company and regularly embody them in your actions and choices. Align your actions with the ideals you demand from your team members. This consistency promotes the significance of those principles and establishes the benchmark for conduct inside the company.

show Integrity and Ethical Conduct: Act with integrity and show ethical conduct in all parts of your career. Uphold high ethical standards, be truthful in your conduct, and make judgments based on what is ethically correct. By showing integrity, you inspire trust and establish a culture where ethical behavior is valued.

Show Accountability and Responsibility: Take accountability for your actions and consequences. Accept responsibility for errors and shortcomings, and display resilience in overcoming problems. By keeping yourself responsible, you set an example for others to take responsibility for their work and results.

Exhibit Strong Work Ethic: Demonstrate a strong work ethic by continually putting in the effort, going above and beyond, and aiming for perfection. Show devotion, tenacity, and a commitment to providing high-quality work. When your team colleagues experience your work ethic, they are more inclined to mimic it in their job.

Foster Open Communication: Encourage open communication by actively listening, appreciating varied opinions, and supporting polite debate. Be friendly and available to your team members, encouraging them to express their views, ideas, and concerns. By demonstrating open communication, you establish a culture of trust, cooperation, and creativity.

Invest in Personal Growth: Continuously invest in your personal growth and development. Seek chances to study, develop new skills, and increase your knowledge. Share your learnings and growth experiences with your team members, highlighting the necessity of continual improvement. By displaying a growth mindset, you motivate others to embrace learning and strive for ongoing progress.

Support and Empower Others: Support and empower your team members to attain their greatest potential. Provide direction, coaching, and resources to help them achieve. Encourage autonomy and distribute duties, enabling people to grow and enhance their abilities. By empowering people, you exhibit your conviction in their skills and develop a culture of trust and cooperation.

Recognize and Appreciate Efforts: Regularly recognize and appreciate the efforts of your team members. Celebrate their successes, milestones, and efforts. Acknowledge their hard work and give constructive criticism. By displaying real gratitude, you promote excellent behaviors and push others to thrive.

Embrace Diversity and Inclusion: Embrace diversity and inclusion within your team and company. Value and respect other viewpoints, backgrounds, and experiences. Create an inclusive atmosphere where everyone feels appreciated and heard. By accepting diversity, you stimulate innovation, creativity, and cooperation.

Maintain a good Attitude: Maintain a good attitude even in hard conditions. Demonstrate resilience, optimism, and a solution-oriented approach. Your optimistic attitude may inspire and encourage others, building a culture of optimism and resilience across the business.

Summary:

Leading by example is a strong leadership style that encourages and inspires others to follow suit. By living the beliefs, actions, and attitudes you demand from your team members, you create credibility, develop trust, and form a healthy workplace culture. Through strategies such as clarifying and embodying core values, demonstrating integrity and ethical behavior, showing accountability and responsibility, exhibiting a strong work ethic, fostering open communication, investing in personal growth, supporting and empowering others, recognizing contributions, embracing diversity and inclusion, and maintaining a positive attitude, leaders can effectively lead by example and create a culture of excellence, trust, and success within their teams and organizations. Remember, your actions speak louder than words, and leading by example is a great tool for successful leadership.

Performance Management

Performance management is a vital part of good leadership that entails establishing clear standards, offering feedback, and supporting the growth of people and teams to attain their greatest level of performance. It involves a variety of tasks, including goal setting, performance review, coaching, and acknowledgment. In this chapter, we will analyze the relevance of performance management and dig into practical techniques for leaders to develop an effective performance management process.

The Importance of Performance Management:

Goal Alignment: Performance management ensures that individual and team goals are linked with the wider objectives of the business. By creating clear and detailed objectives, leaders help employees understand their roles and responsibilities, prioritize their efforts, and contribute to the overall success of the business.

Performance Improvement: Performance management offers a framework for identifying areas of improvement and resolving performance gaps. Through frequent feedback and coaching, leaders may support people in growing their abilities, overcoming problems, and boosting their performance. This technique encourages ongoing learning and progress.

Employee Engagement and Motivation: Effective performance management increases employee engagement and motivation. When people get frequent feedback and appreciation for their achievements, they feel appreciated and driven to work at their best. It fosters a good work atmosphere where individuals feel encouraged and empowered to accomplish their objectives.

Accountability and Transparency: Performance management encourages accountability and transparency inside the company. By defining performance objectives and delivering feedback, leaders create clear standards and hold employees responsible for their outcomes. This procedure guarantees that performance assessments are fair, consistent, and based on objective criteria.

Talent Development and Succession Planning: Performance management plays a key role in talent development and succession planning. By measuring performance, identifying high-potential personnel, and giving development opportunities, leaders may nurture talent inside the business and prepare future leaders for crucial responsibilities. It helps the long-term prosperity and sustainability of the organization.

Techniques for Effective Performance Management:

Set Clear Performance Objectives: Establish clear and explicit performance objectives for individuals and teams. Convey goals, objectives, and key performance indicators (KPIs). Ensure that expectations are aligned with the organization's vision and strategy. By offering clarity, people may concentrate their efforts on obtaining the intended goals.

Provide Ongoing Feedback: Offer frequent feedback to people about their performance. Provide both positive reinforcement for strengths and constructive comments for areas of growth. Feedback should be detailed, timely, and focused on actions and results. This helps people recognize their progress, make corrections, and continue their growth.

Conduct Performance Assessments: Conduct formal performance assessments at regular intervals, such as yearly or biannually. Use a systematic assessment procedure that examines individual performance against set criteria and objectives. Provide a complete review that reveals strengths, areas for growth, and development possibilities. Performance assessments should be objective, fair, and based on facts.

Implement Development Plans:
Develop personalized growth programs based on performance assessments and feedback. Work cooperatively with people to discover areas for growth and build actionable development objectives. Provide resources, training, and coaching to help their growth path. Regularly monitor progress and revise development strategies as appropriate.

Foster a Coaching Culture: Create a coaching culture where leaders serve as coaches, leading and supporting people in their performance and growth. Encourage open and honest conversation, active listening, and asking effective questions. Coaching talks should concentrate on individual development, problem-solving, and unleashing potential.

Recognize and Reward Performance: Recognize and reward great performance to reinforce desirable behaviors and drive people. Celebrate triumphs, milestones, and contributions in meaningful ways. Rewards might include verbal appreciation, monetary incentives, job growth possibilities, or increased duties. Tailor incentives to individual preferences and company culture.

Provide continual Learning Opportunities: Support continual learning and growth by delivering training programs, seminars, and access to resources. Provide opportunities for people to upgrade their abilities, learn new information, and remain informed about industry trends. Encourage participation in conferences, webinars, and online courses. Foster a culture of ongoing learning and professional progress.

Foster Collaboration and Teamwork: Promote collaboration and teamwork inside the company. Encourage people to work together, exchange expertise, and encourage each other's progress. Create possibilities for cross-functional cooperation and information exchange. By promoting a collaborative atmosphere, you boost performance and use the aggregate skills of the team.

Regularly Review and alter objectives: Regularly review and alter objectives to ensure they stay relevant and aligned with changing conditions. Monitor progress, offer comments, and make appropriate revisions to objectives. Agile goal management helps people and teams to adapt and react to altering objectives and market circumstances.

Lead by Example: As a leader, lead by example in your performance and dedication to continual development. Demonstrate a strong work ethic, establish high expectations, and actively participate in your performance management process. By leading by example, you inspire and empower people to take responsibility for their performance and growth.

Summary:

Performance management is a critical part of good leadership, helping firms to align objectives, boost performance, and develop talent. By setting clear expectations, providing ongoing feedback, conducting performance evaluations, implementing development plans, fostering a coaching culture, recognizing and rewarding performance, providing continuous learning opportunities, fostering collaboration, and leading by example, leaders can create a performance-driven culture that inspires individuals to excel. Effective performance management encourages employee engagement, responsibility, and progress, eventually contributing to the success and sustainability of the firm. Remember, performance management is a continuous process that involves effort, communication, and a commitment to helping people in realizing their maximum potential.

Strategic Thinking and Planning

Strategic thinking and planning are important components of good leadership and organizational success. They entail the capacity to anticipate the future, appraise the existing condition, and devise methods to bridge the gap. In this chapter, we will discuss the relevance of strategic thinking and planning and dig into practical techniques for leaders to design and execute successful plans.

The Importance of Strategic Thinking and Planning:

Vision and Direction: Strategic thinking and planning give a clear vision and direction for the company. They assist leaders identify the organization's purpose, values, and long-term objectives. By presenting a compelling vision, leaders motivate their employees and unite efforts toward a single aim.

Anticipating and Adapting to Change: Strategic thinking and planning help leaders predict and adapt to change. They entail studying market trends, detecting new opportunities, and assessing possible hazards. By knowing the external environment and industry dynamics, executives may make educated judgments and adapt strategies appropriately.

Resource Allocation and Prioritization: Strategic thought and planning help leaders distribute resources efficiently. They entail analyzing resource availability, prioritizing efforts, and determining strategic trade-offs. By aligning resources with strategic goals, executives improve resource use and increase the organization's impact.

Innovation and Competitive Edge: Strategic thought and planning drive innovation and provide a competitive edge. They entail discovering market gaps, investigating innovative company strategies, and generating distinctive value propositions. By establishing a culture of innovation, leaders generate creativity, distinctiveness, and sustained development.

Alignment and cooperation: Strategic thinking and planning foster alignment and cooperation within the company. They entail engaging stakeholders, developing cross-functional communication, and generating common objectives. By synchronizing efforts and supporting cooperation, leaders establish a unified and high-performing company culture.

Principles for Effective Strategic Thinking and Planning:

Clarify the Vision and mission: Start by defining the organization's vision and mission. Define the intended future state and the key values that influence decision-making. Ensure that the vision is appealing, inspirational, and linked with the organization's goal.

Conduct a SWOT study: Perform a detailed study of the organization's strengths, weaknesses, opportunities, and threats (SWOT). Assess internal capabilities, market dynamics, competitive environment, and emerging trends. Identify areas of competitive advantage and possible hazards to influence strategic choices.

Set Clear Goals: Set clear and detailed goals that support the organization's vision. Define quantifiable objectives and key performance indicators (KPIs) that match the strategic direction. Ensure that goals are realistic, difficult, and time-bound.

Engage Stakeholders: Engage important stakeholders in the strategic planning process. Seek feedback from workers, customers, partners, and industry experts. Their opinions may bring useful insights and boost the quality of strategic decision-making. Foster a culture of inclusivity and cooperation.

Develop Actionable plans: Develop actionable plans to attain the identified goals. Break down the strategic objectives into concrete initiatives, programs, and action plans. Assign duties, distribute resources, and define timeframes. Ensure that strategies are aligned with the organization's strengths and limits.

Monitor Progress and Adjust: Continuously monitor the progress of strategic initiatives and assess their efficacy. Regularly assess critical performance metrics and milestones. Identify areas of achievement and areas that need modification. Be receptive to criticism and change plans as required to guarantee continued alignment with the changing environment.

Foster a Culture of Learning and Creativity: Create a culture that emphasizes learning and creativity. Encourage innovation, risk-taking, and the sharing of best practices.

Support professional development and offer resources for staff to better their skills and expertise. Foster an attitude of constant development.

Communicate the Strategy: Effectively communicate the strategic strategy across the company. Ensure that all workers understand the strategic direction and their involvement in its implementation. Clearly express the strategic objectives, efforts, and the logic behind them. Provide frequent updates on progress, triumphs, and obstacles. Encourage two-way communication, enabling workers to ask questions, offer feedback, and share ideas. By creating openness and open communication, you build a feeling of ownership and alignment among all stakeholders.

Build Strategic Capabilities: Invest in building the strategic capabilities of the company and its personnel. Provide training and development programs that promote strategic thinking, analytical capabilities, and decision-making ability. Encourage staff to enhance their awareness of the industry, market trends, and upcoming technology. Develop a personnel pool with excellent strategic understanding.

Embrace Continuous Improvement: Recognize that strategic thinking and planning are iterative processes.

Embrace an attitude of constant development. Regularly analyze the success of tactics and make required revisions. Learn from both triumphs and setbacks, exploring chances to enhance and optimize the strategic approach.

Summary:

Strategic thinking and planning are crucial for firms to negotiate the challenges of today's business world and achieve long-term success. By clarifying the vision, conducting a thorough analysis, setting clear objectives, engaging stakeholders, developing actionable strategies, monitoring progress, fostering a culture of learning and innovation, communicating effectively, building strategic capabilities, and embracing continuous improvement, leaders can drive the organization towards its desired future state. Strategic thinking and planning help leaders anticipate change, make educated choices, allocate resources efficiently, develop teamwork, and build a competitive edge. By adopting strategic thinking and planning as a continuous process, firms can adapt, innovate, and succeed in an ever-evolving business environment.

Managing Remote Teams

The development of remote work has provided new problems and possibilities for executives to properly manage their teams. Managing remote teams involves a distinct set of skills and methods compared to standard in-person team management. In this chapter, we will discuss the relevance of managing remote teams and dig into practical techniques for leaders to establish a productive and engaged remote workforce.

The Importance of Managing Remote Teams:

Flexibility and Employment-Life Balance: Remote employment gives flexibility and the chance for workers to attain a better work-life balance. By managing remote teams successfully, leaders can create an atmosphere that meets workers' personal and professional requirements, enabling increased job satisfaction and retention.

Talent Acquisition and Retention: Remote work extends the talent pool, enabling firms to recruit and keep top personnel from anywhere in the globe. Effective management of remote teams helps executives to exploit multiple skill sets and perspectives, leading to enhanced creativity and productivity.

Productivity and Performance: When managed appropriately, remote teams may be incredibly productive. Remote work decreases commute time and lowers interruptions in the workplace, allowing workers to concentrate on their job. Effective management methods may assist maximize productivity and sustain high-performance levels.

Collaboration and Communication: Managing remote teams demands excellent collaboration and communication technologies and processes. By embracing technology and developing clear communication routes, leaders can create seamless collaboration, ensuring that distant team members are connected, informed, and engaged.

Employee Engagement and Morale: Remote employment may often contribute to feelings of isolation and separation. Effective management of remote teams entails actively engaging and supporting team members to maintain high levels of engagement, morale, and a feeling of belonging.

Approaches for Managing Remote Teams:

Set explicit Expectations: Establish explicit expectations about work hours, deliverables, and communication methods. Ensure that team members understand their roles, responsibilities, and performance objectives. Clear expectations offer a platform for responsibility and productivity.

Facilitate Communication: Encourage frequent and open communication among the remote team. Use numerous communication technologies like video conferencing, instant messaging, and project management systems to boost cooperation and retain a feeling of connectedness. Schedule frequent team meetings, one-on-one check-ins, and virtual social events to develop connections.

Provide the Right Tools and Resources:
Equip remote team members with the essential tools and resources to accomplish their tasks. Provide access to project management tools, collaboration platforms, and other digital solutions. Offer training and assistance to ensure team members can use these technologies effectively.

Foster a Positive Team Culture: Create a positive team culture that encourages trust, openness, and cooperation.

Encourage team members to discuss ideas, offer feedback, and encourage one another. Celebrate accomplishments, acknowledge achievements, and develop a feeling of camaraderie among the remote workforce.

Support Work-Life Balance: Recognize the significance of work-life balance for remote team members. Encourage them to develop boundaries between work and personal life. Be flexible with scheduling and meet individual requirements when feasible. Support their well-being by fostering self-care and stress management.

Provide Continuous Development possibilities: Offer possibilities for professional development and progress for remote team members. Provide access to online training, webinars, and tools that fit with their professional aspirations. Encourage skill-building and continual learning to increase their knowledge and contribute to the organization's success.

Emphasize Results and Outcomes: Focus on results and outcomes rather than micromanaging distant team members. Trust them to perform their tasks and give help when required. Evaluate performance based on goals and objectives rather than the number of hours done.

Be Responsive and Available:
Be responsive and accessible to remote team members. Promptly react to their inquiries, give direction, and answer concerns. Ensure that they feel supported and respected, especially while working remotely.

Promote Social engagement: Create chances for social engagement among distant team members. Encourage virtual team-building activities, such as online games, virtual coffee breaks, or casual chat channels. Foster a feeling of community and togetherness, even when team members are physically far.

Regularly review and Adjust: Regularly review the efficacy of your management tactics for remote teams. Seek input from team members and make improvements as required. Continuously review the team's performance, communication, and cooperation to find areas for improvement and execute adjustments appropriately.

Summary:

Managing remote teams demands a proactive and strategic strategy to promote productivity, engagement, and successful cooperation. By setting clear expectations, facilitating communication, providing the right tools and resources, fostering a positive team culture, supporting work-life balance, offering continuous development opportunities, emphasizing results and outcomes, being responsive and available, promoting social interaction, and regularly evaluating and adjusting management strategies, leaders can effectively manage remote teams and create a cohesive and high-performing virtual workforce. With the correct methods and support, remote teams may flourish, generating exceptional outcomes while enjoying the advantages of remote work flexibility.

Employee Recognition and Rewards

Employee recognition and rewards play a key part in building a healthy work environment, motivating workers, and boosting overall productivity. Recognizing and rewarding workers for their successes and contributions not only recognizes their hard work but also promotes desirable behaviors and increases morale. In this chapter, we will analyze the relevance of employee recognition and incentives and dig into practical techniques for leaders to establish successful recognition and reward programs.

The Importance of Employee Recognition and Rewards:

Motivation and Engagement: Employee recognition and prizes are significant motivators that foster employee engagement. When workers feel recognized and respected for their contributions, they become more devoted to their job and the business. Recognition and awards create a feeling of purpose, leading to increased levels of work satisfaction and productivity.

Retention and Loyalty: Recognition and awards contribute to employee retention and loyalty. When workers feel acknowledged and rewarded for their achievements, they are more likely to stay with the firm and remain loyal. This decreases turnover and the related expenses of recruiting and training.

Performance Improvement: Recognizing and praising people for their successes may boost performance levels. It provides positive reinforcement, motivating personnel to continue generating great achievements. By recognizing and rewarding outstanding performers, leaders motivate others to strive for perfection, establishing a culture of continual progress.

Reinforcement of desirable Behaviors: Employee recognition and awards help promote desirable behaviors and values inside the company. When workers are praised for showing behaviors consistent with the organization's goal and values, it encourages others to follow suit. This maintains a healthy work culture and helps develop the ideal organizational standards.

Team Collaboration and Morale: Recognition and awards may build a collaborative and good work atmosphere. When workers are acknowledged for their cooperation and collaboration, it develops connections and creates a feeling of togetherness. It promotes team spirit and motivates workers to support and elevate one another.

Techniques for Effective Employee Recognition and Rewards:

Timely and Specific Acknowledgment: Provide timely and specific acknowledgment to workers for their successes. Acknowledge their efforts as soon as possible to reinforce the good effect of their acts. Be precise in emphasizing the actions, talents, or results that lead to their acknowledgment, indicating that their contributions are appreciated and acknowledged.

Tailor appreciation to Individual Preferences: Recognize that workers have diverse preferences when it comes to appreciation. Some may embrace public acclaim, while others prefer more intimate kinds of gratitude. Take an effort to learn each employee's preferences and adapt recognition appropriately. This guarantees that the acknowledgment is relevant and well-received.

Create a Culture of Peer Recognition: Encourage a culture of peer recognition where workers may acknowledge and appreciate their peers. Implement initiatives or platforms that promote peer-to-peer appreciation and encourage workers to actively engage. This promotes a friendly and inclusive work atmosphere where workers feel valued by their colleagues.

Align Recognition with Organizational Values:
Ensure that the recognition and awards correspond with the organization's beliefs and goals. Tie recognition to actions and results that represent the intended values and objectives of the company. This underlines the significance of living up to the organization's objective and develops a feeling of purpose among personnel.

Offer a Variety of awards: Provide a choice of awards to appeal to varied employee preferences. This may include monetary incentives, non-monetary prizes like gift cards, additional time off, professional development opportunities, or public recognition. Offering varied awards helps workers to pick prizes that are most relevant to them, enhancing their happiness and motivation.

Encourage Managerial Recognition: Encourage managers to actively acknowledge and respect their team members. Train and empower managers to properly deliver recognition and awards. This not only enhances the manager-employee connection but also sets a great example for the rest of the company.

Foster Continuous Feedback: Integrate recognition and incentives into continuous feedback and performance talks. Regularly offer positive comments to staff, noting areas of improvement and development potential. Additionally, take these occasions to acknowledge and celebrate workers' successes and growth. This generates a feedback-rich atmosphere where recognition becomes an intrinsic component of the feedback and growth process.

Make acknowledgment Visible: Make acknowledgment visible and available to the whole organization. Utilize communication channels like newsletters, bulletin boards, or company-wide emails to disseminate tales of staff successes and accolades. By making acknowledgment public, you establish a culture of gratitude and motivate others to strive for greatness.

Encourage Employee Input: Involve workers in the recognition and incentives process. Seek their opinion on the forms of recognition and awards they find significant. This may be done via surveys, focus groups, or suggestion boxes. By integrating workers into the decision-making process, you improve their feeling of ownership and participation in the award program.

review and Adjust: Regularly review the success of your recognition and incentive programs. Assess their influence on employee motivation, engagement, and performance. Gather input from workers and supervisors to identify areas for improvement. Adjust your methods as required to ensure that the recognition and rewards efforts stay relevant and meaningful.

Summary:

Employee recognition and awards are key components of a flourishing and engaged team. By creating successful recognition and incentive programs, management may encourage workers, increase performance, develop a great work culture, and enhance employee retention. Through timely and specific recognition, tailored approaches, peer recognition, alignment with organizational values, offering a variety of rewards, encouraging managerial recognition, fostering continuous feedback, making recognition visible, involving employee input, and regularly evaluating and adjusting programs, leaders can create a culture of appreciation and recognition that drives organizational success. Investing in employee recognition and awards is an investment in the well-being and contentment of your workers, leading to higher productivity and a good work environment.

Workforce Diversity and Inclusion

Workforce diversity and inclusion have become essential considerations in developing successful and sustainable enterprises. Embracing diversity implies appreciating and integrating people from diverse origins, cultures, experiences, and opinions into the workforce. Inclusion, on the other hand, entails building an atmosphere where all workers feel appreciated, respected, and have equal opportunities to participate and thrive. In this chapter, we will discuss the value of workforce diversity and inclusion and dig into practical solutions for leaders to build a varied and inclusive workplace.

The Importance of Workforce Diversity and Inclusion:

Enhanced Innovation and Problem-Solving: Diversity brings together people with varied views, ideas, and experiences. By nurturing a diverse workforce, firms may draw into a broad variety of perspectives and approaches to problem-solving. Different origins and viewpoints inspire inventive thinking, resulting in unique solutions and a competitive advantage in the marketplace.

Improved Decision-Making: A varied and inclusive workforce helps decision-making processes. When a diversity of views and ideas are examined, choices are more well-rounded and complete. varied teams are more likely to evaluate a larger variety of possibilities and make educated judgments that represent the requirements and preferences of a varied client base.

Increased Employee Engagement and Retention: A workplace that celebrates diversity and supports inclusion develops a feeling of belonging and engagement among workers. When people feel welcomed, appreciated, and included, they are more likely to be devoted to the company and driven to do their best. This, in turn, leads to greater staff retention rates and lower turnover.

Access to a Larger Talent Pool: A commitment to diversity and inclusion extends the talent pool from which firms may recruit. By aggressively soliciting applicants from different backgrounds, companies have access to a greater variety of talents, experiences, and viewpoints. This helps them to recruit top individuals and establish high-performing teams that drive organizational success.

Enhanced Organizational Reputation: Organizations that embrace diversity and inclusion build a favorable reputation. They become renowned as inclusive employers that embrace diversity, justice, and equality. This reputation not only attracts great personnel but also helps develop good connections with customers, stakeholders, and the wider community.

Techniques for Fostering Workforce Diversity and Inclusion:

Create Inclusive Policies and Procedures: Establish policies and procedures that encourage diversity and inclusion at all levels of the company. This involves assessing recruiting and hiring procedures to guarantee fairness and avoid prejudice, creating diverse applicant slates, and ensuring equitable chances for professional promotion and development.

Develop Diversity Training and Education: Provide diversity and inclusion training to all workers to improve awareness and foster understanding. This training should concentrate on detecting unconscious biases, comprehending diverse views, and developing inclusive actions and language. Ongoing education initiatives may assist staff in consistently increasing their awareness of diversity and inclusion.

Foster a Culture of Inclusion: Build a culture where all workers feel appreciated, respected, and included. Cultivate frank communication, active listening, and respectful relationships among team members. Celebrate diversity by understanding and accepting other cultures, experiences, and opinions. Foster cooperation and teamwork to establish an inclusive workplace where everyone's contributions are recognized.

Implement Diversity Metrics and Tracking:
Establish diversity metrics to assess progress and evaluate the effect of diversity and inclusion programs. Collect data on workforce demographics, representation, and inclusion indicators to identify areas for improvement and assess achievement. Regularly review and report on these indicators to hold leaders responsible and encourage continual progress.

Establish Employee Resource Groups: Encourage the development of employee resource groups (ERGs) that bring together persons with common experiences or interests. ERGs offer a venue for networking, support, and advocacy inside the company. They add to a feeling of belonging and allow workers to participate in diversity and inclusion efforts.

Encourage Diverse Leadership: Promote diversity in leadership roles within the company. Encourage the growth and progression of people from different backgrounds into leadership positions. By having diverse leaders at the helm, companies may show their commitment to diversity and inclusion while also benefitting from a greater variety of viewpoints and experiences in decision-making processes.

Foster Cross-Cultural Competence: Encourage workers to acquire cross-cultural competence and sensitivity. Provide chances for cultural exchanges, training programs, or mentoring projects that assist workers get a greater understanding of diverse cultures and viewpoints. This develops empathy, lowers prejudices, and allows successful cooperation in a diverse work setting.

Foster External Collaborations: Establish collaborations with external organizations and groups that promote diversity and inclusion. Collaborate with diverse suppliers, participate in industry events focused on diversity, and engage in community activities that benefit underrepresented groups. These relationships not only contribute to a more varied environment but also strengthen the organization's reputation as an inclusive workplace.

Regularly Assess and Adjust: Regularly assess the efficacy of diversity and inclusion programs. Gather input from workers, perform surveys, and participate in focus groups to understand their perspectives and find areas for improvement. Use this input to make required improvements and constantly develop the organization's approach to diversity and inclusion.

Leadership Accountability: Hold leaders responsible for supporting diversity and inclusion within their teams and throughout the company. Incorporate diversity and inclusion objectives into performance assessments and give leaders the necessary tools and assistance to promote inclusive work environments. By stressing leadership responsibility, companies may guarantee that diversity and inclusion remain key focus.

Summary:

Fostering worker diversity and inclusion is not just the ethical thing to do but is also crucial for organizational success in today's globalized and diversified corporate world. By embracing diversity, firms may unleash the full potential of their staff, generate innovation, and strengthen decision-making. Inclusive workplaces enhance employee engagement, retention, and a healthy business culture. By implementing strategies such as creating inclusive policies and practices, providing diversity training, fostering a culture of inclusion, tracking diversity metrics, establishing employee resource groups, promoting diverse leadership, fostering cross-cultural competence, fostering external partnerships, regularly assessing and adjusting, and holding leadership accountability, organizations can build diverse and inclusive workforces that thrive in an ever-evolving world.

Personal Growth and Self-Reflection

Personal development and self-reflection are vital components of being a great boss and leader. They entail a constant process of self-awareness, self-improvement, and self-discovery. In this chapter, we will examine the role of personal growth and self-reflection in leadership, look into practical tactics for personal development, and highlight the advantages of creating a growth mindset.

The Importance of Personal Growth and Self-Reflection:

Self-Awareness: Personal progress starts with self-awareness — recognizing one's strengths, shortcomings, values, and beliefs. Self-aware leaders are more prepared to make deliberate decisions, control their emotions, and engage successfully with others. They have a greater grasp of their influence on the team and can change their leadership style appropriately.

Continuous Learning: Personal progress needs a commitment to continual learning. Exceptional leaders are driven to develop their knowledge, abilities, and competence. They explore chances for professional development, attend seminars or conferences, read books, and participate in self-study to keep up-to-date with industry trends and best practices. By continually learning, leaders may offer new insights and unique ideas to their employees.

Adaptability: In a continuously changing corporate environment, personal development is vital for leaders to adapt and succeed. Through self-reflection, leaders may discover areas where they need to improve and acquire new capabilities. They may welcome change, seek new challenges, and stay adaptable in their approach to leadership. Adaptable leaders motivate their people to accept change and promote a culture of continual progress.

Empathy and Emotional Intelligence: Personal development cultivates empathy and emotional intelligence in leaders. Through self-reflection, leaders acquire a better knowledge of their own emotions and those of others. They get better at detecting and regulating emotions, displaying empathy, and developing genuine relationships with team members. This boosts their capacity to encourage, assist, and inspire their team to achieve remarkable achievements.

Resilience: Personal development enhances leaders' resilience in the face of hardship. By reflecting on prior experiences and learning from obstacles, leaders acquire the resilience required to manage challenging circumstances. They can bounce back from losses, retain a good attitude, and motivate their team to persist. Resilient leaders establish a culture of resilience, where setbacks are recognized as chances for progress.

Strategies for Personal Growth and Self-Reflection:

Set Clear objectives: Identify precise objectives for personal growth and development. These objectives might be focused on areas such as increasing communication abilities, developing emotional intelligence, or gaining new leadership qualities. Set quantifiable targets and build a strategy to attain them. Regularly evaluate and adjust your objectives as you move on your personal development path.

Seek input: Invite input from peers, mentors, and team members. Feedback gives useful insights into your strengths and opportunities for progress. Actively listen to input, think about it, and take necessary action to rectify any gaps or areas of improvement. Embrace constructive criticism as a chance to learn and improve.

Practice Self-Reflection: Carve out regular time for self-reflection. This may be via writing, meditation, or peaceful contemplation. Reflect on your experiences, choices, and relationships with others. Consider what happened well, what might have been done better, and what lessons you can take from each event. Self-reflection helps you develop clarity, understand your principles, and make meaningful decisions.

Cultivate a Growth mentality: Develop a growth mentality, thinking that your talents and intellect can be developed through work and practice. Embrace difficulties, persevere in the face of setbacks, and consider failures as chances for learning and progress. Emphasize constant learning and progress in yourself and create a growth mentality in your team.

Seek Development Opportunities:
Look for chances inside your business or elsewhere that may help your personal development and self-reflection:

-Job Rotations: Explore the potential of rotating into new jobs or divisions within your business. This helps you to obtain a better knowledge of the industry, develop new talents, and increase your network.

-Cross-Functional Projects: Volunteer to engage in cross-functional projects or initiatives. Collaborating with colleagues from other departments exposes you to fresh viewpoints and helps you gain new abilities while contributing to the organization's objectives.

-External Courses and Certifications: Consider enrolling in external courses or seeking certifications that fit with your career objectives. These programs give organized learning opportunities and recognized qualifications that may boost your knowledge and reputation in particular areas.

-Secondments or Exchanges: Explore options for temporary assignments or exchanges with partner organizations, industry groups, or even foreign postings. These experiences expose you to new cultures, work settings, and ways of doing things, extending your horizons and developing your talents.

-Peer Learning and Mentorship: Engage in peer learning and seek out mentors or advisers who may give direction and assistance. Peer learning groups or mentoring programs enable you to learn from the experiences and knowledge of others, giving useful insights and recommendations for your improvement.

-Contribute to Professional Communities: Actively engage in professional communities, forums, or online groups about your field. Engaging in debates, exchanging thoughts, and seeking advice from other professionals may broaden your network, expose you to various viewpoints, and give you continual learning opportunities.

-Remember, identifying growth opportunities is a continual process that needs proactivity and a dedication to constant learning. Be open to new experiences, accept difficulties, and actively seek out chances that correspond with your personal and professional development objectives. By regularly exploring growth opportunities, you may improve your knowledge, abilities, and network, and continuously progress as a leader.

Summary:

Personal development and self-reflection are crucial components of being an extraordinary leader. By finding development opportunities, you actively engage in your progress and continually increase your knowledge, abilities, and viewpoints. Whether via work rotations, cross-functional initiatives, external courses, secondments, online learning, mentoring, or contributing to professional forums, each opportunity provides a possibility for development and learning. Embrace these possibilities, be interested, and be devoted to your growth. As you increase your talents and widen your perspectives, you not only become a more successful leader but also inspire and empower people around you. The road to personal growth is a lifetime quest, and by actively pursuing development opportunities, you may consistently progress and make lasting influence in your leadership journey.

Conclusion

"The Exceptional Boss: Secrets to Becoming a Great Leader" is a thorough book that dives into numerous elements of leadership, giving useful insights and practical tactics to help people become great bosses. Throughout the book, we have explored topics such as developing a leadership mindset, effective communication, inspiring and motivating others, building trust and authenticity, emotional intelligence, decision-making, and problem-solving, building high-performing teams, leading through change, coaching and mentoring, work-life balance, effective delegation, conflict resolution, building a positive company culture, leading by example, performance management, strategic thinking, and planning, managing remote teams, employee recognition and rewards, workforce diversity and inclusion, personal growth and self-reflection, and many more.

By implementing the ideas and practices presented in this book, readers will have the skills and knowledge to lead with excellence, establish a great work environment, and propel their teams toward success. The book highlights the value of continuing personal and professional growth, as well as the relevance of creating good connections, supporting teamwork, and accepting change.

Becoming a great boss is a process that needs self-awareness, ongoing learning, and a dedication to improvement. It requires adopting successful leadership methods, building emotional intelligence, and inspiring people to attain their greatest potential. By learning the secrets presented in this book, readers will be well-equipped to manage the obstacles of leadership, inspire their teams, and have a positive effect on their businesses.

"The Exceptional Boss: Secrets to Becoming a Great Leader" offers a helpful resource for anyone desiring to better their leadership abilities, whether they are new to leadership positions or seasoned professionals. By adopting the ideas and insights from this book, readers may build the attitude, abilities, and attributes necessary to become outstanding bosses who inspire, motivate, and lead with integrity.